IMAGES
of America

SAN FRANCISCO'S
PARKS

The San Francisco Recreation and Park Department's iconic sign was introduced in 1930 and is attributed to architect Gardner Dailey. The bracket is a signature Mission Revival–style element. It was a product of the playground department, which, at that time, was newly renamed as the recreation department. In recent years, the sign has been duplicated, minus the post's round base cap, and is used in many parks. (Courtesy of History Center, San Francisco Public Library.)

ON THE COVER: This 1930s photograph of Funston Playground, now called Moscone Recreation Center, shows some of the many uses of an urban park. In the foreground is the tot's sandbox area, which is enclosed by seating for attending parents, and just behind are tennis and other courts. All this is against a backdrop of apartment buildings lining Bay Street in the surrounding residential Marina District. (Courtesy of San Francisco Recreation and Park.)

IMAGES
of America

SAN FRANCISCO'S
PARKS

Christopher Pollock

ARCADIA
PUBLISHING

Published by Arcadia Publishing
Charleston, South Carolina

Printed in the United States of America

Library of Congress Control Number:

For all general information, please contact Arcadia Publishing:
Telephone 843-853-2070
Fax 843-853-0044
E-mail sales@arcadiapublishing.com

Visit us on the Internet at www.arcadiapublishing.com

*To all those who have volunteered their time over the decades
to assist the San Francisco Recreation and Park Department
in maintaining the city's many parks. By participating in this,
these unheralded helpers have spread their spirit of sharing.*

CONTENTS

ACKNOWLEDGMENTS

It has been my privilege since becoming the first historian in residence for the San Francisco Recreation and Park Department to have the experience of bringing the department's storied history to light. A shout-out goes to the department's general manager, Phil Ginsburg, for approving this extracurricular project. Without the help of both Susan Goldstein and Tim Wilson of the History Center at the San Francisco Public Library, this project would not have seen the light of day. Additional help came from Jeremy Menzies of the San Francisco Metropolitan Transit Authority; Charles Kennard; Ashley Summers, who is the liaison for San Francisco Recreation and Park Commission; and the Library of Congress. And finally, I would like to recognize all the unidentified photographers who captured these images of a time and place so many decades ago.

INTRODUCTION

The City and County of San Francisco has a myriad of properties administered by the San Francisco Recreation and Park Department. Numbering 230 properties, they occur by water, on hilltops, in open rolling areas, or intimate pockets between buildings. They include parks, playgrounds, miniparks, open spaces, a yacht harbor, and community gardens. Over time, the department has developed more than just places to recreate. Many of these places have been host to active and passive programs, which enrich the mind, body, and spirit—and are places to have some fun.

Not all recreation spaces within San Francisco are administered by the recreation and park department. Some others are overseen by city departments including the Port Commission, San Francisco Public Works, San Francisco Public Utilities Commission, or the State of California. In some cases, there are shared responsibilities with these other entities. The Presidio is a separate federally administered space as are all the areas encompassing the Golden Gate National Recreation Area (GGNRA).

Prior to the existence of the City and County of San Francisco, as well as the preceding Spanish and then Mexican rule, the area was originally inhabited by the Yelamu, an independent tribe of the Ramaytush Ohlone peoples. When the City and County of San Francisco was incorporated in 1850, the first municipal property identified as an outdoor communal space was Portsmouth Square, where the nucleus of government was situated. All the city's property boundaries were calculated from dead center of the square.

Early San Francisco chronicler Frank Soulé noted the following in his 1854 book, *Annals of San Francisco*: "There seems no provision for a public park—the true lungs of a large city." Soulé scolded that early official maps showed that every square vara (the Spanish unit of land measure still in use at the time) was slated for building lots. In addition to Portsmouth Square, only three squares had been planned as recreation space for the town. The three earliest maps of the city, completed by surveyors Jean-Jacques Vioget (1839), Jasper O'Farrell (1847), and William M. Eddy (1849), had projected only the following two additional open spaces: Union Square and Washington Square, both gifts to the city in 1850 from John White Geary, the first mayor of newly American San Francisco. Columbia Square was a third.

Several parks were a product of the Van Ness Ordinance of 1855–1856, which was enacted by the common council (the governing body prior to the board of supervisors). Part of its mission was to reserve land and secure land titles for public purposes, including parks. This was voided, but in 1858, the state legislature confirmed the terms of ordinance. With their inclusion ratified, some parks were named, in a patriotic gesture, for a past US president or important person in the country's creation.

The following is a chronological summary of how parks came to be by looking at the various incarnations of departments that ultimately grew into what is known today as the recreation and park department.

From 1850 to 1899, any squares, the name for the city's early parks, such as Portsmouth Square, were administered by the city's department of streets, sewers, and squares (DSS) with its own board. During this period of the city's rapid growth, the DSS had far greater practical concerns to attend to before addressing any green or recreation space as we know it today. In 1848, San Francisco had a population of some 1,000, which swelled to more than 149,400 by 1870.

District improvement clubs were a huge force in getting parks developed in the city's early years (and continue to be). As a residential tract was developed by new parcel owners, those residents banded together to request the infrastructure to serve their neighborhood's needs and desires.

Not all was smooth sailing to develop these parks. Land ownership squabbles, such as those surrounding the ownership of land for Alamo Square, Holly Park, Jackson Park, and especially, Lafayette Park, were common in the 19th century. In the latter example, it was former city attorney Samuel Holladay who claimed that he owned the eastern half of the park since 1851; however, the city claimed it was in public ownership. Starting in 1863, Holladay started fencing his claim, which included six parcels that bordered Clay Street between Octavia and Gough Streets. He built a two-story Victorian Italianate–style residence with barn and windmill for himself in 1869, calling it Holladay Heights. Considered a squatter by the city, he was sued four times, and each time, the city lost to Holladay's cleverness. The city lost out, and a large multistory apartment building was ultimately constructed, which remains today.

A subperiod of note was between 1870 and 1899. In parallel to the DSS, a new park commission was created under state jurisdiction, and its board was appointed by the Governor. This was created with the inception of Golden Gate Park, Buena Vista Park, and Mountain Lake Park, an act of the California legislature known as Order No. 800. The first board consisted of Pres. David W. Connely, Samuel F. Butterworth, Charles F. MacDermott, and Andrew I. Moulder as secretary.

An important event in Golden Gate Park's cultural development was a byproduct of the 1894 California Midwinter International Exhibition. The fair was held due to there being what was called a panic (recession) and promoters hoped to bring business to the city. It was a success. After the fair closed, the landscape of the central racetrack-shaped bowl remained and became the site called the Music Concourse that would be host to today's de Young Museum (first opened in 1895), Japanese Tea Garden (1895), Spreckels Temple of Music (1900), and California Academy of Sciences (1916).

The next period of growth was from 1900 to 1907. With a sweeping city charter revision in 1900, the DSS was abolished, the department of public works was its replacement, and most of the city's parks were now administered by the single governing park commission, which came under city and county jurisdiction, not the state. The park commission's board was now appointed by the mayor. That board consisted of five men and a secretary; one board member was mandated to be an artist who would oversee aesthetic decisions. Sculptor M. Earl Cummings was chosen to fill the role.

During the period from 1908 to 1931, the playground commission was created by a city charter amendment, which was carried out in 1908. This commission was a separate but parallel entity from the park commission—with limitations. The newly created playground commission's first members were as follows: Henry J. McCoy (secretary, Young Men's Christian Association), Joseph C. Astredo (superintendent, Cathedral Mission of the Good Samaritan), Sidney S. Peixotto (manager, Columbia Park Boys' Club), Thomas F. Boyle (president, board of education), Margaret S. Hayward (civic department of the California Club), and Laura White (first president, California Club). Despite this, not all playgrounds were under this commission's jurisdiction—yet. It would take years for the park commission to hand over the more recreational sites to the playground commission.

The background to this development is that in 1906 the Playground Association of America was incorporated. The California Club was a local progressive women's reform organization in the forefront of the playground movement. The commission's first order of business was creation of the North Beach (now Joe DiMaggio) Playground.

The next grouping of years is from 1932 to 1949. In the fall of 1931, during the Great Depression, voters approved a city charter amendment that allowed creation of the arts commission, charged to oversee all the city's aesthetic decisions. The impact to the park department was that since another department would oversee design, the mandated artist was no longer required to sit on the park commission.

With voter approval, an amendment to the city charter allowed a renaming the playground commission. In a January 1932 meeting, the playground commission changed the nomenclature to be the recreation commission, a term which covered a broader interpretation of the commission's responsibilities. This was spurred by action of the Playground and Recreation Association of

America (originally the Playground Association of America), which broadened its scope by 1930 to include physical fitness, recreation, sports, performing arts, research, training institutes, personnel services, and site visits.

One of the largest periods of growth was, ironically, during the fiscally dark days of the Great Depression of the 1930s when the federal government created the Works Progress Administration (WPA), which established federally funded jobs. With much foresight, the city acquired much land during this period for recreational development. Many parks and playgrounds benefitted from the toil of thousands of WPA laborers who either built entirely new parks or added to the existing ones.

During World War II, San Francisco was an important US port in the Pacific Ocean theater and several park sites were commandeered for use by troops. Most of the Funston Playground (now George Moscone) was home to the US Army for use by the San Francisco Army Port of Embarkation. Here, barracks were constructed to augment those in Fort Mason, located across the street.

The Crocker Amazon Playground became Navy Fleet Hospital No. 113. The four huge quadrangles of the playground's lawn were commandeered in 1944 by the Navy for the siting of prefabricated steel and plywood hospital buildings. The hospital specialized in the rehabilitation of wounded Navy and Marine Corps. With the war ended in 1945, returning veterans found it difficult to find housing. The relatively new buildings were repurposed as living quarters for veterans and their families, and in January 1947, the quarters were turned over to the San Francisco Housing Authority for leasing. At its maximum, the site held some 3,000 occupants in 744 apartments, ranging in size from a studio up to three bedrooms. These remained well into the postwar period.

The most prominent was in the civic center where, starting in 1941, temporary barracks, used as lodging for visiting military personnel, occupied the plaza. Initially, there were six buildings, but four more were in filled over time. The formal gardens were all removed due to construction of these buildings. After their removal in 1946, a simpler landscape was left than had previously existed.

In 1946, a member of the board of supervisors launched a program titled "Master Plan for Youth," which included all the city's agencies concerned with the care and development of children. The main goal was the prevention of juvenile delinquency. Josephine Randall, recreation director, was cited as a major contributor to the program; one of the outcomes was voter approval of Proposition No. 6 in the fall of 1947, which was for $12 million to fund recreation bonds. Post–World War II was to become the second period of unprecedented growth in parks. A staggering number of projects were funded including 39 recreation centers, 19 gymnasiums, 6 indoor swimming pools, 18 new and the renovation of 13 existing playgrounds, development of 2 beaches, the junior museum, and enlargement of the city's municipal Camp Mather.

The last period covered is from 1950 to the present. In November 1949 voters approved the consolidation of the recreation department with the park department, which passed with 54 percent; the consolidation went into effect in July 1950. The new department was called the San Francisco Recreation and Park Department, which is unlike every other city in the United States, which usually called it park and recreation department. The board was now a total of seven, plus a secretary.

The idea of community gardens came about during World War I and became larger during World War II. One example was in 1942 when the Crocker Amazon Playground partly used. There were many unofficial communal garden spaces across the city on unused sites. One example is Clipper Community Garden, which was started about 1940 when Virginia and Edward Paige moved to the area from Tennessee, and she started growing their own food on the vacant lot. Over time, such spaces became more difficult to find. The movement to codify them as official properties was developed in 1973 with the political support of supervisor Robert Mendelsohn and others to make San Francisco land more life-giving. The project was closely tied to the Alvarado Neighborhood Arts Program and specifically to sculptress Ruth Asawa, who believed that gardens should be part of the program. Today, some are freestanding while others have been developed within an existing park.

In 1968, the newly elected administration of Mayor Joseph L. Alioto is cited to have brought a federally funded program to San Francisco for the implementation of a new program for the creation of miniparks. Discussion within the San Francisco Recreation and Park Commission started that

February about the idea of miniparks, and later that year, the commission approved the mechanism to start the process of building 16 miniparks with Resolution No. 7696. The resolution was to fund an initial work order to the city's real estate department for $16,000, which was for title search and appraisal fees related to 13 properties. The parks were to be funded by a matching, 50-50 basis with the federal government. Soon after, the nonprofit organization Friends of Recreation and Parks was organized to bolster funding and outreach to the community.

The Golden Gate National Recreational Area (GGNRA) was created in 1972 as a federally administrated entity. Several maritime-oriented properties previously administered by the recreation and park department were ceded over time to the GGNRA, including Ocean Beach, Sutro Park, Lands End, Phelan Beach, Aquatic Park, and portions of Lincoln Park.

Today, those spaces administered by the San Francisco Recreation and Park Department include an ever-widening variety of recreation opportunities included within its portfolio of parks, playgrounds, miniparks, open spaces, and community gardens. In the past several years, these spaces have become host to newly appreciated active sports including disc golf, skate boarding, and pickleball. A game of bubble soccer can be seen on occasion as well. Safety and accessibility for all have also become the norm in most parks today.

In 2017, San Francisco was cited as the nation's first city to have every resident live within a 10-minute walk to a park. The percentage was calculated by the Trust for Public Land, a national nonprofit that facilitates the creation of parks and whose team analyzes park systems for the nation's 100 largest cities.

This book has been organized into eight chapters, each that groups photographs with a common broad theme. Each chapter is laid out chronologically, so it shows a progression of stylistic and programmatic changes over time. There is a common ground between Chapter One: Parks and Playgrounds and Chapter Two: Recreation Centers. Chapter One is an overall view of many properties, while Chapter Two has a focus on the buildings within some of the department's properties. The very focused Chapter Three: Play Structures is a detailed review of the variety of play apparatus that has been installed in parks over time. More passive recreational pursuits are covered in Chapter Four: Activities. Chapter Five: Athletics shows the extensive active sports and related activities that have taken place. The next one, Chapter Six: Special Places shows many points of interest, while Chapter Seven: Events shows specific events and their date. Finally, there is Chapter Eight: Before or During Development, which illustrates a site before or in process.

Most of the photographs shown were taken for the department between roughly 1925 and 1992. They are not being presented here as representing all the department's properties. Rather they are just a sampling of the historical photograph holdings recently deacquisitioned to the History Room of the San Francisco Public Library by the department. The History Room is the official archive of all city materials.

While most of the photographs shown come from files of the department's publicity department (now known as communications) several photographs included here come from a series of seven leather-bound binders with gold-embossed lettering on the covers. These were created under the direction of Josephine D. Randall, who was superintendent of the recreation department from 1926 until her retirement in 1951. They seem to have been created to show the department's achievements during the earlier part of her 25-year tenure. Unfortunately, there is no labeling on the interior pages, just numbers for the photographs, which have no known key legend. Many of the locations shown are recognizable while some have had to be forensically assessed for key clues such as a building in the background. One, of Oceanview Playground, was taken so early that it was only by identifying a school building (long since demolished) in the shot that became the starting point for identification. There are several others that will take deeper sleuthing to figure out their location.

One

PARKS AND PLAYGROUNDS

As seen looking north in 1851, just a year after incorporation of the city, this is Portsmouth Square, the hub of early San Francisco. Looking at the buildings lining Washington Street, some of the businesses shown are a restaurant, printer, pharmacy, newspaper, and a theater. The landscape is yet to be developed. By 1856, the square was fenced and fully landscaped in a formal style. (Courtesy of Library of Congress.)

The racetrack-shaped South Park was originally a fashionable privately held gated park for the residences that faced it. Serving 68 lots, the park opened in 1854 and was similarly designed to those in London, England. The garden was planted with trees, shrubs, and flowers. With the demise of the area's status, the park was purchased in 1895 for use by all city residents. (Courtesy of History Center, San Francisco Public Library.)

The apex of this hill, seen from Jackson Street, was once a quarry for material to pave the city's streets. Although Alta Plaza was a product of the Van Ness Ordinance of 1855–1856 as a public park, its ownership was contested, and settlement was not achieved until 1888. The distinctive south-facing terraces were constructed starting in 1900 to tame the very steep sandy hillside. (Courtesy of San Francisco Municipal Transportation Authority Photo Archive.)

Mission Playground and Pool was established in 1913 on board of education property that housed the Marshall Primary School, which moved elsewhere. This photograph shows the rear of the clubhouse and its pool structure, which was built in 1916. The playground was yet to be developed, not having much other than a lawn area at the time. (Courtesy of History Center, San Francisco Public Library.)

The park department's first ties to Lake Merced came in 1922 when the Spring Valley Water Company, owners of the Lake Merced Rancho property, agreed to lease 170 acres for a period of 15 years to be used as a municipal golf course. The city then acquired the property in 1930 when Spring Valley was purchased, creating the basis of today's Public Utilities Commission. (Courtesy of San Francisco Recreation and Park.)

The Crocker Amazon Playground was a huge flat property originally intended as a city water reservoir but continued to be used for truck farming until taken over by the recreation commission. Construction occurred between 1934 and 1937 by workers from the federally funded WPA, a program of the Great Depression. They excavated and graded the landscape for 11 baseball fields and installed a sprinkler system. Bleachers with locker and storage rooms under them were constructed using cast-in-place concrete. Additionally, six tennis courts, two basketball courts, and two small playgrounds were built. Related work included the construction of paths, drives, gutters, retaining walls, and landscaping. The sum spent on the project was $938,869. (Courtesy of History Center, San Francisco Public Library.)

Today's Gilman Playground was initially called Gilman Beach. In 1933, during the throes of the Great Depression, $7,500 was approved to purchase the land. Crews dug out the property's hillside with pick, shovel, and wheelbarrow. In 1935, the WPA finished construction of the boathouse, pier, and toilet building; additionally, riprap was placed to armor the shoreline. (Courtesy of History Center, San Francisco Public Library.)

In Pacifica is Sharp Park, home to an 18-hole golf course designed by Alister MacKenzie and H. Chandler Egan. MacKenzie was the designer of the famed Cypress Point Club course, among many others. The course was sculpted using sand pumped from the adjacent beach, and loam was spread on top to facilitate grass growth. The course was officially dedicated in 1932. (Courtesy of History Center, San Francisco Public Library.)

The original acreage of the spectacular gorge of Glen Canyon Park was purchased in 1924. The multiuse recreation center, a product of the WPA, was completed in 1938. Architect William Merchant designed it and included a reference to a barn that was previously on the site. The building's overall massing recalls the Swedish pavilion at the Panama-Pacific International Exhibition in 1915. (Courtesy of History Center, San Francisco Public Library.)

Southside Playground, renamed in 1930 as Father Crowley Playground, is no longer extant. It was decommissioned in 1953 for construction of the Bayshore Highway connection to the San Francisco–Oakland Bay Bridge, and the Hall of Justice sits on much of the property today. It was a major hatching ground for major and minor league baseball players. The baseball backstop was auctioned off in 1957. (Courtesy of San Francisco Recreation and Park.)

The steep hillside site of Douglass Playground was formerly the site of a quarrying operation. (Much of the dressed stone facing of McLaren Lodge in Golden Gate Park is faced in stone from this quarry.) The playground's lower portion, shown here with its clubhouse, was initially dedicated in 1928. Ongoing work would be performed by the WPA and was completed in 1936. (Courtesy of History Center, San Francisco Public Library.)

Landscaping above Douglass Playground's upper terrace has just been completed. Other tasks included excavation of blasted loose rock, construction of rubble walls, laying irrigation and drainage pipe, erection of fencing, erection of a standard convenience station, and construction of a baseball field. It was opened in 1938 with Mayor Angelo Rossi in attendance. (Courtesy of San Francisco Recreation and Park.)

The Rossi Playground annex, located across Edward Street, was originally constructed for board games and had several horseshoe pitching courts. (There were also other venues for the pitching sport in the Mission District, Stern Grove, and Golden Gate Park.) The convenience building, one of several similar ones, was designed by architect William Merchant and had distinctive zigzag design grilles over the windows. (Courtesy of History Center, San Francisco Public Library.)

Here, the Upper Noe Valley Recreation Center Building has just been finished. The project, dedicated in 1957, included a gymnasium with regulation court and two practice courts with seating, meeting rooms, kitchen, office, toilets, and an auditorium. Outside there were playground areas with a baseball diamond, tennis courts, volleyball, basketball courts, and two tot lots. Donald B. Kirby was the building's architect. (Courtesy of History Center, San Francisco Public Library.)

This c. 1940 photograph looks at the southwest corner of the Helen Wills Playground, which was where the playground portion was located. At the extreme right is the clubhouse that was once located in the playground's northwest corner. The balance of the playground was a series of various sport courts. Later, the playground was slightly narrowed to allow for construction of the adjacent Broadway Tunnel. (Courtesy of History Center, San Francisco Public Library.)

The land for Ward Recreation Center, previously called Oceanview Playground, was purchased from multiple parties; in 1922, the board of supervisors purchased the first lots, which were turned over to the playground commission. Additional land was purchased by 1931. Architect Gardner Dailey designed the initial layout; the gently south-sloping land was divided into two levels with its undulating retaining wall. (Courtesy of San Francisco Recreation and Park.)

The States Street Playground was the first of several elements developed on Corona Heights Hill. The terrace where the playground is sited was previously where the Gray Brothers brick factory was located. Labor funded by the WPA helped to create the flat terrace and the first portion was the tennis courts in 1937, and the playground, which remains intact today, followed in 1949. (Courtesy of History Center, San Francisco Public Library.)

San Francisco voters approved Proposition No. 6 in November 1947, which was for $12 million to fund recreation bonds. With the funding, recreation centers were built or enlarged throughout the city. The virtually landlocked site for Cow Hollow Playground was purchased in 1948. With the Modernist-style recreation building designed and completed by William Merchant, the park was dedicated in 1951. (Courtesy of History Center, San Francisco Public Library.)

Five properties were purchased in 1917 to create Rolph Playground. The park was dedicated in 1922 with some 4,000 children in attendance who demonstrated games and athletics. Mayor "Sunny Jim" Rolph, who was born and raised in the immediate area, was also in attendance as the guest of honor. In 1938, the WPA constructed bleachers in the baseball field. (Courtesy of History Center, San Francisco Public Library.)

The Visitacion Valley Playground first opened in 1933 with a clubhouse designed by architect Gardner Dailey. This photograph shows the second clubhouse, which opened in 1953 and was designed by architect William Merchant. It contained a clubroom, office, kitchen, storage, and toilet rooms. Outside there was a tot area and a separate area for older children with swings, slides, and a softball diamond. (Courtesy of History Center, San Francisco Public Library.)

Property for the Richmond Playground was originally assigned by the city for use by the Benevolent Ladies' Protection and Relief Society, which was established to render assistance to dependent women and children. The site went unused and was transferred to the playground commission in 1914. In 1916, some initial work was done, and many years later, the clubhouse was dedicated in 1951. (Courtesy of History Center, San Francisco Public Library.)

The opening of Peixotto Playground took place in 1951 in a celebration headed by Mayor Elmer Robinson. The Rocky Mountain Participation Nursery School holds sway in the clubhouse building today. The school began in 1948 when it was known as Mission Cooperative Nursery School. It was located on Capp Street, near Potrero Avenue, before it moved to its present location in the 1970s. (Courtesy of History Center, San Francisco Public Library.)

Land to construct the Eureka Valley Recreation Center was acquired by the purchase and demolition of 22 buildings. Construction was delayed due to material shortages related to the Korean War. The building, opened in 1956, included an auditorium and gymnasium, offices, and a kitchen. The exterior work included a softball field, tennis and basketball courts, and a tot play area. (Courtesy of History Center, San Francisco Public Library.)

Laurel Hill Playground was once a part of Laurel Hill Cemetery, a 55-acre cemetery that contained an estimated 35,000 remains. After the cemetery was closed and the remains moved, the land was turned over to residential development during the 1940s and 1950s. The playground opened on May 5, 1955. The architects for the project were Paul A. Ryan and John Michael Lee. (Courtesy of History Center, San Francisco Public Library.)

The three-story Recreational Arts Building opened in Duboce Park in 1957 as a facility devoted to music, drama, dance, and photography. These divisions had been previously spread out around the city in various facilities. The Modernist-style building was designed by architects William Mooser Jr. and John W. Gloe. (Courtesy of History Center, San Francisco Public Library.)

With residential growth of the Cayuga Terrace District in the 1940s, Cayuga Playground was developed with a series of acquisitions including purchases and a transfer. Construction was funded by the November 1947 bond, Proposition No. 6, which allotted $12 million for improvement and enlargement of existing and acquisition of new playgrounds, as well as construction of new buildings. The park was opened in 1951. (Courtesy of History Center, San Francisco Public Library.)

The Lakeside District, clustered around Ocean Avenue, was constructed as a residential development between 1936 and 1950. City voters approved the selling of bonds in 1947 to incur indebtedness for building out several projects, which included Junipero Serra Playground in this suburban setting. The 1,800-square-foot clubhouse was designed by architect William Mooser. The facility opened on January 18, 1955 (Courtesy of History Center, San Francisco Public Library.)

In March 1928, the initial parcel of land was given by the Archdiocese of San Francisco for the creation of St. Mary's Playground. Additional land was purchased, and the playground was then developed between 1930 and 1933. The labor was provided by the federally funded WPA. Later, the giant Quonset hut–form building, containing an auditorium, gym, and clubrooms, was opened in 1951. (Courtesy of History Center, San Francisco Public Library.)

The West Portal Playground sits on top of the like-named subterranean streetcar station. The playground was opened in 1931 with a tennis court and playground across the park's east end. The clubhouse, shown here, was constructed in 1951 but was later demolished due to reconstruction of the San Francisco Municipal Railway (MUNI) station below. A replacement clubhouse was constructed and opened in 1979. (Courtesy of History Center, San Francisco Public Library.)

Union Square was one of the city's earliest parks. Initially, the land was a large dune—a far cry from what is seen today. Over time, the sand was removed to level the area. The park's name came from its early use as a Civil War–era rallying point where orators gathered the public and argued for California as a state of the Union. (Courtesy of History Center, San Francisco Public Library.)

Looking down from Coit Tower in Pioneer Park shows a crowded day on the top of Telegraph Hill in the 1960s. At the center is the statue of Christopher Columbus, installed in 1957. The hill was first known as Signal Hill when a flagpole with large arms was installed in 1846 to announce the arrival of ships in San Francisco Bay. (Courtesy of San Francisco Municipal Transportation Authority Photo Archive.)

Bayview Park, seen here in 1960, does not look much different today as it still awaits its turn to be developed. The property was created as a park in 1915. Some work was done during the Great Depression when the Works Progress Administration funded construction of roadways, gutters, a retaining wall, and the planting of thousands of trees, mostly eucalyptus. (Courtesy of History Center, San Francisco Public Library.)

In 1971, the Greek-style amphitheater opened in McLaren Park with a seating capacity of 1,200. It was designed by Architect Alex Yuill-Thornton. In 2005, the venue was named for Jerry Garcia. Garcia (1942–1995) was the Grateful Dead band's singer, songwriter, and guitarist who spent his boyhood years living at 87 Harrington Street in the nearby Excelsior District. (Courtesy of History Center, San Francisco Public Library.)

Seen in this c. 1980 photograph is the upper south portion of Mission Dolores Park where there was an amoeba-shaped wading pool, which was built around 1909. Here, the pool has been filled with sand, which became the play equipment area with swings, jungle gym, and slide. Additionally, there was a boat donated by the US Navy in 1975. (Courtesy of San Francisco Recreation and Park.)

The newly completed urban landscape of St. Mary's Square is shown here in 1957 after a parking garage with 800-spaces was constructed underneath. The park was designed by landscape architect Robert Royston, who separated the various spaces using low walls. An existing row of poplar trees was retained as a soft backdrop, while the existing sculpture of Sun Yat-Sen provided a focal point. (Courtesy of History Center, San Francisco Public Library.)

This aerial shot shows George Christopher Playground soon after it was completed in 1971. Shown surrounding the playground is an entirely new subdivision called Diamond Heights, which was the last part of the city to be built out with its housing, parks, and shopping. In the distance is another part of the infrastructure, St. Nicholas Antiochian Orthodox Church. (Courtesy of History Center, San Francisco Public Library.)

Facing the Hyde Street cable car tracks is the Hyde-Vallejo Minipark. The board of supervisors approved the mid-block parcel purchase cost of $84,000 in 1971. The Department of Housing and Urban Development paid half the cost as part of a federally funded program. The sloping site, a meandering and terraced space, opened in 1972. (Courtesy of History Center, San Francisco Public Library.)

Here, Portsmouth Square is seen soon after the land was completely excavated for an underground parking garage. The notion of a parking garage constructed under the square was first discussed in 1946. But not until 1962 was the 800-car garage dedicated. The garage cost was $3.2 million. Fireworks, a staple of Chinatown dedication events to scare evil spirits, were ignited during the festivities. (Courtesy of History Center, San Francisco Public Library.)

Two

RECREATION CENTERS

Prior to the Mission Playground and Pool Building, the site was used as a private school, which burned in the 1906 Earthquake and consequent fire. The playground department acquired the property, and a recreation building with pool opened in 1916. Its distinctive Mission Revival style used an archway form for the main entry and roof gable ends as a signature unadorned pediment form. (Courtesy of History Center, San Francisco Public Library.)

The Moscone Recreation Center clubhouse was completed in 1924 for $30,000. It was designed by John Reid Jr., who was the city architect at the time. The English half-timbered-style building with stucco infill contained a basketball court, office, toilets, and a community room. In 2008, an addition to the north side was dedicated with members of the Moscone family attending. (Courtesy of History Center, San Francisco Public Library.)

Property for the Chinese Playground, now known as the Willie "Woo Woo" Wong Playground, was purchased in 1925, which consisted of a series of buildings on nine contiguous parcels that once occupied the inter-block street. With demolition of the buildings, the playground was dedicated in early 1927 as a trilevel landscape with swings, slides, and courts for tennis, volleyball, and basketball. (Courtesy of History Center, San Francisco Public Library.)

Land for the Excelsior Playground, consisting of almost two-thirds of the block, was purchased by the board of supervisors for the playground commission in 1911. A small clubhouse was initially built but shown here is the second clubhouse on the site, which was built in 1927. The H-shaped building contained an auditorium with stage, club room, kitchen, and five showers; it cost $11,000. (Courtesy of History Center, San Francisco Public Library.)

Today's Hayes Valley Playground was previously where the Victorian-era Simpson Memorial Church sat at the intersection of Hayes and Buchanan Streets. It became surplus after mergers with other congregations formed Temple Methodist Episcopal Church. In 1928, representatives from the Hayes Valley Merchants and Property Owners Association requested a playground, and by the end of 1930, the recreation center was opened in the existing church. (Courtesy of San Francisco Recreation and Park.)

Sharp Park has the unusual attribute of being located within San Mateo County. Shown here is the Honora Sharp Golf Clubhouse that was built in 1931 by the San Francisco Construction Company for $19,959. In 1936, an addition was built for a restaurant. That phase was a project of the federally funded Works Progress Administration. (Courtesy of San Francisco Recreation and Park.)

An early use of the property where Glen Canyon Park was established was as the first commercial manufacturing plant for dynamite in the United States. In 1868, the Giant Powder Company began production under exclusive license from Alfred Nobel. On the evening of November 26, 1869, an explosion destroyed the entire facility, killing two men and injuring several others. (Courtesy of San Francisco Recreation and Park.)

Originally, Cabrillo Playground was property assigned to the board of education, but it was turned over to the playground commission and combined with an additional lot purchase. The field house building was constructed using SERA (State Emergency Relief Administration) labor. It was probably designed by Gardner Dailey, who was architect for the Rochambeau clubhouse. Mayor Angelo Rossi dedicated the playground in 1938. (Courtesy of History Center, San Francisco Public Library.)

Property for Fulton Playground was obtained in a 1938 swap with the board of education who required land at Balboa Park for development of the junior college there, now known as San Francisco City College. Architect Gardner Dailey likely designed this clubhouse as it is like another he designed. Construction labor was provided by the federally funded WPA, and the playground opened in 1939. (Courtesy of San Francisco Recreation and Park.)

The Senior Center Building in Golden Gate Park is living its third life. The Renaissance Revival-style building was designed by architects Weeks and Day and opened as the Golden Gate Park District Police Station in 1932. Then, it was rededicated as the San Francisco Police Academy in 1937. The building became a senior center in 1965, and in 1980, it was rehabilitated. (Courtesy of History Center, San Francisco Public Library.)

Land for Argonne Playground was originally assigned to the board of education but was transferred to the playground commission in 1925. (The name comes from the Forest of Argonne, France, which was the site of several military battles during World War I.) The playground opened in 1926. A new clubhouse was dedicated in 1953 with a club room, office, kitchen, and storage space. (Courtesy of History Center, San Francisco Public Library.)

Ten years after this photograph was taken in 1951, the same view of what is now known as the Minnie and Lovie Ward Recreation Center in the Ocean View-Merced Heights-Ingleside (OMI) District, was used as a background to the short documentary film called *Ask Me, Don't Tell Me*. It illustrated how San Francisco gang members could contribute to society by working on community service projects. (Courtesy of History Center, San Francisco Public Library.)

The 21,000-square-foot Joseph Lee Recreation Center was designed by architect William Merchant. The U-shaped building contained a gymnasium, clubroom, auditorium, offices, locker rooms, and storage. The project was funded by the 1947 voter approved Proposition No. 6, which funded a $12 million bond issue for the improvement and expansion of recreation throughout the city. Mayor Elmer Robinson dedicated the building in 1951. (Courtesy of History Center, San Francisco Public Library.)

The Potrero Hill Recreation Center, designed by architect William Merchant, is in the form of a giant Quonset hut. The form was popularized during World War II for its efficient structural capability, which achieved a wide span. It was dedicated in 1951 with Mayor Elmer Robinson in attendance. The festivities were accompanied by Scottish bagpipers and included folk dancing and an exhibition basketball game. (Courtesy of History Center, San Francisco Public Library.)

Requests to establish a playground in the vicinity of the intersection of Foote and Cayuga Streets from the Cayuga Improvement Club and the Southern Council of Civic Clubs were received in 1940. The upshot was dedication of the Cayuga Playground in 1951, which included a clubhouse, landscaping, tennis and basketball courts, baseball diamond, and playground equipment. Architect William Merchant designed the clubhouse. (Courtesy of History Center, San Francisco Public Library.)

The land for Merced Heights Playground was acquired from the Pacific Coast Construction Company for the sum of $15,660 in 1947. With the rise of residential construction in the area came the need for infrastructure like this playground. The design by architect William Merchant included three terraces in the west-facing terraced hillside. (Courtesy of History Center, San Francisco Public Library.)

What was originally a board of education property, was transferred to the recreation department. Called the Chinese Center, the 22,000-square-foot, three-story concrete building, was dedicated in 1951. It contained a gymnasium, craft rooms, auditorium, basketball and volleyball courts, and play areas. A replacement building, now known as the Betty Ann Ong Chinese Recreation Center, was dedicated on the same site in 2012. (Courtesy of History Center, San Francisco Public Library.)

In the northeast corner of Stern Grove is the Wawona Clubhouse, which was dedicated in 1949. Today, it is used by Project Insight, a division of the recreation and park department, which serves the hearing-impaired and vision-impaired communities of children, teens, and young adults. Its nearby playfield has, in the past, been used for lawn bowling, putting, and croquet games. (Courtesy of History Center, San Francisco Public Library.)

The J.P. Murphy Playground was originally called the Ortega Playground. Depression-era Works Progress Administration workers built the ball game courts sometime between 1935 and 1938. The playground commission renamed the playground for J.P. Murphy, a former park commissioner, in 1941. The fieldhouse's construction was approved in 1941 but did not commence due to a materials shortage. The building was dedicated in 1951. (Courtesy of San Francisco Recreation and Park.)

The initial piece of land for Silver Terrace Playground was purchased in 1943, and two others were added by 1951. The playground with its clubhouse was dedicated later that year. In 1956, bleachers, like those also being constructed in Funston Playground at the time, were constructed for the baseball field. A bronze plaque was dedicated to William "Pop" Edwards in 1964. (Courtesy of History Center, San Francisco Public Library.)

Land for the Junipero Serra Playground was purchased in 1951 as part of the growing Lakeside District that was built by the Stoneson Development Company, which touted the project as a "garden community of small [not inexpensive] homes." In this suburban setting, the playground's 1,800-square-foot clubhouse was designed by architect William Mooser, and the playground was dedicated in 1955. (Courtesy of History Center, San Francisco Public Library.)

At the west edge of Duboce Park is the Recreational Arts Center Building (now Harvey Milk Center for the Arts) that was opened in 1957. The center pulled together many different but related program disciplines into a single central facility for the first time including music, drama, dance, and photography. (Courtesy of History Center, San Francisco Public Library.)

The Funston Senior Recreation Center on the Moscone Recreation Center grounds was an existing building that was enlarged and rededicated in 1959. Mayor George Christopher attended its dedication and then stepped to the adjacent putting green for an unofficial match. It was an informal center where attendees socialized, played cards, and made music together. It was not part of the city's senior program. (Courtesy of History Center, San Francisco Public Library.)

The beginning of the Hayes Valley Playground was when, in 1955, the church building on the site was deemed inadequate as a facility. The neighborhood was sorely in need of a playground, especially with construction of the Hayes Valley Apartments that were about to be constructed for low-income renters nearby. The upshot was new playground and clubhouse that were dedicated in 1959. (Courtesy of History Center, San Francisco Public Library.)

The third tennis clubhouse to be built on this Golden Gate Park site was named for William M. Johnson, a US representative in the Davis Cup Challenge during 1920–1927 with a record 13 wins and 3 losses. The Midcentury-style building, faced in brick, was designed by architect Leonard S. Mosias and was dedicated in 1959. It was demolished in 2019. (Courtesy of History Center, San Francisco Public Library.)

Silver Tree Day Camp in Glen Canyon Park was established by the recreation department in 1941 as a summer program to expose city children to the benefits of the country. Originally, there was no building, but rather tents were set up to accommodate the day campers. Shown here is the permanent building that was constructed in 1961 using Second Bay Area design principals. (Courtesy of History Center, San Francisco Public Library.)

George Christopher Playground was a new playground that was dedicated in 1971 as part of the city's Diamond Heights development project. The plan was first approved by the board of supervisors in 1955. Architect Arthur Lee of the San Francisco Bureau of Architecture designed the clubhouse building. Installed inside the building were a trio of whimsical ceramic wall murals sculpted by Peter VandenBerge. (Courtesy of History Center, San Francisco Public Library.)

Three

PLAY STRUCTURES

The later 19th-century wood gondola-style swings in the Sharon Quarters for Children (now Koret) in Golden Gate Park could seat up to four children. Given the chance, the children could propel themselves using the inertia of their bodies and feel the sensation of flying. This portion of an 1890s stereoview also shows the playground's first carousel that was under a fabric tent structure. (Author's collection.)

Fleishhacker Playfield opened in 1925 with many amusements for children. In the background is the domed building housing the carousel. There were rides on the Little Puffer steam train and live animals. Surrounding the giant round sandbox are gondola and other type swings, teeter totters, Ferris wheel, and slide. Off-camera and to the right are the Mother's Building and other amenities. (Courtesy of San Francisco Municipal Transportation Authority Photo Archive.)

The playground area of Fleishhacker Playfield, the genesis of today's San Francisco Zoo, included a double-corkscrew slide. The manufacturer, C.W. Parker Amusement Company, claimed it to be "the only one in the world" in their advertising. (They also manufactured a single version for the Sharon Playground in Golden Gate Park.) The other rides included an airplane, Ferris wheel, and merry-go-round. (Courtesy of History Center, San Francisco Public Library.)

Seen in the 1940s, the Margaret Hayward Playground, with its Mission-style clubhouse, has a full range of play equipment including a double slide, single hang rings, swings, teeter totter, and a rectangular sandbox. (Most city playground sandboxes were a hexagonal form.) Note the Victorian style residences in the background, which were all removed in the well-meaning urban renewal efforts of the mid-20th century. (Courtesy of San Francisco Recreation and Park.)

The modernized version of the older wood gondola-style swing, also seen in the Sharon playground, is shown here in the Fleishhacker Playfield, now the San Francisco Zoo. Its sculptural quality using formed metal tubing exploits the pure geometric form of a circle and reflected the modern approach to metal play equipment around the mid-20th century. (Courtesy of History Center, San Francisco Public Library.)

On the east slope of Mount Davidson is the Miraloma Park residential subdivision. Located next to the Miraloma School is the Miraloma Playground, which was dedicated in 1954. Rather basic by today's standards, the playground was funded by the $12 million 1947 recreation bond and contained swings, slides, merry-go-round, and sandbox. In the background was a temporary school building, which opened in 1941. (Courtesy of History Center, San Francisco Public Library.)

The Hayes Valley Playground was developed on a former church property that was leased as a recreation site in 1930. Dedication of this incarnation took place in 1959, with members of the Hayes Valley Parents' Club in attendance who organized efforts to get the new playground built. Along with the standard metal pipe structures, there was also the standard cast-in-place hexagonal sandbox. (Courtesy of San Francisco Recreation and Park.)

Located in the playground at Moscone Recreation Center (previously Funston) was this concrete turtle climbing sculpture. It is representative of forms that could be found in many US playgrounds constructed during the 1950s through the 1980s and San Francisco had several. A cluster still exist, most notably, in McLaren Park near the tennis courts. They were designed by Michigan-based sculptor Jim Miller-Melberg. (Courtesy of History Center, San Francisco Public Library.)

Gilman Playground was initially a product of the later Depression era. In 1968, contractor A. and J. Shooter, Inc., was awarded the rehabilitation project. The work consisted of grading, landscaping, and irrigation. Also, there was standard play equipment used plus a large sand play area with a full-figure cast concrete porpoise and another companion play structure in the form of a turtle. (Courtesy of History Center, San Francisco Public Library.)

The corner site of Howard-Langton Minipark was the site of a one-story factory. The land was acquired in 1970. The minipark was built out with a newer generation of wood and metal playground equipment. Later, a mural was painted on the side of an adjacent building. In 1995, the site was redeveloped as a community garden by the San Francisco League of Urban Gardeners. (Courtesy of History Center, San Francisco Public Library.)

The last buildout of a city hilltop area was when the Diamond Heights District was created between 1961 and 1981. Part of the development's infrastructure was the Christopher Playground. It opened in 1971 with Modernist sculptor David Arron's perforated metal "Pleasure Dome" and Jim Miller-Melberg's cast concrete "Saddle Slide and Playwall" structures among others. These elements were repurposed in the playground's 2021 rehabilitation. (Courtesy of History Center, San Francisco Public Library.)

The Sunnyside Playground clubhouse, as well as adjacent play area, was dedicated in 1971. This after years of requests since 1947 to locate a playground here. The building was named for Mary Margaret Casey, who was a park commissioner from 1958 through 1964. Beyond the usual use of wood poles in the playground was the use of sculptural concrete climbing forms set in the sandscape. (Courtesy of History Center, San Francisco Public Library.)

The park known today as Precita Park was originally named Bernal Park in 1894. Play equipment was installed in the park in 1972 when the local firm Beckwith and Langsner was contracted. The firm designed and installed a slide, bridges, tunnels, twisted metal spaghetti jungle gym, and "a large pig-shaped climbing thing" painted in psychedelic colors, which was all designed by Jay Beckwith. (Courtesy of History Center, San Francisco Public Library.)

The tradition of having a real decommissioned jet plane in Larsen Park as a play structure started in 1958. This was a Vietnam-era supersonic Vought F-8C Crusader. It was helicoptered into the San Francisco Zoo from the Alameda Naval Air Station and then towed to the park in 1975. It was a donation of the US Navy's USS *Coral Sea* aircraft carrier. (Courtesy of San Francisco Recreation and Park.)

The start of Prentiss Minipark, located on a steep hillside, was when Supervisor Robert Mendelsohn recommended the unbuilt lot, originally slated to be a street in an 1861 subdivision map, as the site of a park in 1968. The Bernal Heights District park was partially constructed using telephone poles as a building material. (Courtesy of History Center, San Francisco Public Library.)

The newly reopened Mary B. Connolly Playground (now Koret) in Golden Gate Park was dedicated in 1978. The complete renovation included the addition of a large geometric climbing structure that was made up of metal tubes, connectors, and panels. The configuration provided a wide variety of interesting places to climb or be enclosed within. The playground was designed by landscape architect Michael Painter. (Courtesy of History Center, San Francisco Public Library.)

In the James Rolph Playground was a late Midcentury structure where children could climb in many different directions. This was typical of the playground equipment available in the 1970s and 1980s. This product, using a geometric form in modular units, was designed by Richard Dattner in 1976 and are known as cuboctahedra. These could be once seen at South Park's playground as well. (Courtesy of History Center, San Francisco Public Library.)

One of the benefits of hilly San Francisco is that an in-ground slide can be constructed using the topography. This double and curved concrete slide is part of the Koret Playground in Golden Gate Park. Others can be experienced today in Seward Minipark and Youngblood-Coleman Playground. (Courtesy of History Center, San Francisco Public Library.)

This project was a response to the crowded conditions at the Chinese Playground near the intersection of Stockton and Sacramento Streets. Shown here soon after it opened in 1951, the now rebuilt Chinese Recreation Center is called the Betty Ann Ong Chinese Recreation Center. The former building had a playground on the roof with a variety of metal and wood play apparatus. (Courtesy of History Center, San Francisco Public Library.)

With the work financed through Open Space funds and by the Friends of Noe Valley, which donated the new futuristic climbing apparatus, Noe Valley Courts playground was rededicated in 1981. The jungle-gym play structure consisted of geometric forms molded from transparent Lexan plastic. The assembled modular elements looked like blown bubbles floating through the air. A child could crawl on and through the three-dimensional shapes. (Courtesy of Charles Kennard.)

In 1984 a tot lot was dedicated in the Portsmouth Square playground. It featured six concrete animal sculptures based on Chinese astrology. The figures included representations of a rabbit, tiger, dragon, serpent, ram, and monkey. The artist was Mary Fuller McChesney, who was commissioned by the San Francisco Arts Commission. Funding came from the Mayor's Office of Community Development and the Tamrack Foundation. (Courtesy of History Center, San Francisco Public Library.)

Four

ACTIVITIES

One of the recreation department's classes was in dance. Here, shown in Stern Grove, is a group of girls displaying what they have learned about teamwork, coordination, movement, and creating a memorable scene. (Courtesy of San Francisco Recreation and Park.)

Within the designated girls', or west, half of the Margaret S. Hayward Playground was the clubhouse with its columns and tile roof, which was built in the later 1920s. Here children are dressed for Halloween in costumes probably of their own making as part of the recreation program. Tennis courts and a playground were built here as well. (Courtesy of San Francisco Recreation and Park.)

There was plenty of open land for children to lay out and plant gardens behind the Junior Museum, now the Josephine Randall Junior Museum, when it was initially located where City College of San Francisco is located today. The area had, in the city's early days, been pastureland, and the immediate site was occupied initially by the Ingleside Jail. (Courtesy of San Francisco Recreation and Park.)

60

A performance in front of the Margaret S. Hayward Playground clubhouse is the result of selecting a script, the making of puppets, and rehearsals. This was just one of the recreation commission's many programs designed to teach children while at play. Like a park scene in Paris even today, an audience of young and old gather around the portable theater to watch. (Courtesy of San Francisco Recreation and Park.)

Here is a closeup view of another puppet show being presented in a portable theater. Puppets are useful tools in the development of children; kids can not only participate in the making of puppets but also can have fun bringing their creations to life with providing voices, not necessarily their own, and movement. (Courtesy of San Francisco Recreation and Park.)

The elemental craft of soap carving is an inexpensive and easy medium to learn skills. The idea of subtractive removal is the opposite of creating a form using daubs of clay, which is additive. These are learning concepts that can be transferred to ways of thinking. It can be a bridge to being a sculptor, or at least to appreciating the intent. (Courtesy of San Francisco Recreation and Park.)

Framing and sheathing a plywood boat takes considerable skill in following plans and directions to the letter in the achievement of constructing a maritime-worthy craft. This is shown in the original Junior Museum that was sited where City College of San Francisco is located today. (Courtesy of San Francisco Recreation and Park.)

The study of botany, or plant science, augmented the gardening done at the Junior Museum, now Josephine Randall Junior Museum, when it was first located on Ocean Avenue, now the site of City College of San Francisco. Field trips were taken to collect flowers in the wild. The children pressed the specimen until they were dried and then mounted them for examination. (Courtesy of San Francisco Recreation and Park.)

On the home front, during and after World War II, model airplanes were popular. This started with a 1942 request by the US Navy for high school students to give the war effort an assist by building 500,000 model planes to be used in training Naval air troops. The Junior Museum (now Randall) assisted by creating a model plane recreation program. (Courtesy of San Francisco Recreation and Park.)

Staged on one of the terraces in Stern Grove among towering eucalyptus trees is a promotional ballet scene. It may have been part of one of the many annual Summer Carnivals produced by the recreation department to launch the season of public performances there. These showcases included folk dancing, orchestra music, choral, and specialty numbers. (Courtesy of San Francisco Recreation and Park.)

Prior to World War II and into the war, Moscone Playground, then known as Funston Playground, was one the sites of a kite-flying festival where many boys and girls competed for prizes in various categories. Here, two boys display their elaborate creation in the form of an octagon. Kites were of interest due to wartime aviation design advances. (Courtesy of History Center, San Francisco Public Library.)

Woodworking is just one of the many programs that has been offered by the Josephine D. Randall Junior Museum for many decades. Here, a young girl displays her woodworking project in this c. 1985 photograph. Woodworking teaches manual dexterity, working safely with tools, as well as the nature and limitations of working with wood. (Courtesy of San Francisco Recreation and Park.)

The Sharon Building, part of the original Children's Quarters in Golden Gate Park, has been host to a variety of public craft classes since 1968. The program includes arts education for people of all ages in ceramics, leaded and fused glass, jewelry, metal arts, drawing, painting, and mixed media. Shown here is an example of a student's work in leaded glass around 1985. (Courtesy of San Francisco Recreation and Park.)

In 1935, the recreation department started a photograph arts division, now part of the Harvey Milk Center for the Arts in Duboce Park. After several moves, the division moved into the current Recreational Arts Center, opened in 1957. The separate photograph center occupied the entire basement level. A huge darkroom, the largest in the West at the time, remains in place today. (Courtesy of History Center, San Francisco Public Library.)

Ceramics was one class available at the Josephine Randall Junior Museum. Learning to manipulate clay is a craft requiring many layers of hands-on knowledge. The skill of turning clay on a moving manual foot-turned wheel, which spins, is especially a challenge to master. Beyond the throwing of a pot on a wheel, there are many aspects to learn about glazes and different firing techniques. (Courtesy of San Francisco Recreation and Park.)

Music was part of the many programs at the Recreation Arts Center at 50 Scott Street, today's Harvey Milk Center for the Recreation Arts. Here, musicians are led in the auditorium by a conductor who is training several students to follow the music's time and keep together. The conductor also interprets and conveys the spirit of the music through gestures, uniting the ensemble. (Courtesy of San Francisco Recreation and Park.)

In the 1980s, computers were just becoming a tool for business to be used in many ways. The key element in training was to understand computing basics. The Randall Junior Museum sponsored computer classes, and shown here is probably an Apple II, introduced in 1977. Since Silicon Valley was nearby, many tech companies donated computers for the training of children in the kindergarten-through-12th-grade range. (Courtesy of San Francisco Recreation and Park.)

Five

ATHLETICS

The field known as Big Rec in Golden Gate Park was initially developed for the 1894 Midwinter Fair where parades were held almost daily. Its broad and flat expanse allowed for a cinder track and general athletic grounds, which were later developed primarily for baseball. Today, the baseball fields still remain, and the west baseball diamond is named for Charles H. Graham and the east one for James J. Nealon. (Author's collection.)

Now named Jose Coronado Playground, this playground was originally called Folsom. Its instigation came from the Mission Street Merchants Association, San Francisco Labor Council, and Education, Parks, and Playground Committee of the Board of Supervisors that endorsed an additional playground for this area. In 1927, the playground was opened and included a clubhouse, playing courts, and baseball field. (Courtesy of History Center, San Francisco Public Library.)

One of the many recreational activities in Glen Canyon Park was inclusion of the baseball diamond. Shown in the 1940s with Elk Street in the background, the diamond was part of the original layout when the park was dedicated in 1938. Later, in 1991, the diamond was named for volunteer coach Thelma Williams by the recreation and park department. (Courtesy of History Center, San Francisco Public Library.)

The original baseball diamonds of Moscone Recreation Center were once dominated by the omnipresent 102-foot-high gas storage tank. This is shown in the 1950s in what was then called Funston Square. Later, Diamond No. 1, located in the northwest corner, remembered Edward "Spike" Hennessey and was dedicated in 1958, and No. 2, located in the northeast corner, was dedicated as Eddie Garrigan Field in 1962. (Courtesy of History Center, San Francisco Public Library.)

The availability of baseball fields has been an important part of the department's mission to get children engaged and give them some form of exercise that is fun. These students are part of a latchkey program where recreation centers were open to children if working parents could not be available at home when school closed. (Courtesy of History Center, San Francisco Public Library.)

A clever funding strategy for an outdoor pool was used at the North Beach Playground, today's Joe DiMaggio Playground. After the calamitous 1906 Earthquake and Fire, subterranean cisterns were constructed by the fire department throughout the city to quench fires. It was successfully argued that a pool could double as a cistern. This pool opened in 1911, and its successor remains today. (Courtesy of San Francisco Recreation and Park.)

The prior use of the Mission Playground and Pool was for the Marshall Primary School, constructed after the 1906 Earthquake. After the school moved elsewhere, the playground's pool opened in 1916. It was funded like the one in North Beach a few years earlier, using the same firefighting cistern idea. This pool remains today as the only public outdoor pool in the city. (Courtesy of San Francisco Recreation and Park.)

Garfield Square was designated as a public park in 1881. In 1912, a playground was proposed to be added and some 50 some citizens protested who felt that the grounds should remain as a placid park. Many years later the indoor heated pool was dedicated in 1957, and the event featured exhibitions by local Olympic stars Ann Curtis Cuneo and Delia Meulenkamp. (Courtesy of History Center, San Francisco Public Library.)

Land for the Angelo J. Rossi Playground was formerly home to the Odd Fellows Cemetery. Its pool building was constructed as the third enclosed municipal pool in the city and was dedicated in 1957 by Mayor George Christopher. There was Art Deco–style lettering cast into the pool building's entry. The pool and building were designed by architect H.C. Baumann. (Courtesy of History Center, San Francisco Public Library.)

The Sunset District land, now known as Parkside, for Larsen Park was donated to the city by citizen Carl G. Larsen. The park was developed and dedicated in 1926, and the enclosed pool building was dedicated in 1958. It was designed by architect William Merchant and constructed of steel and wood, which ultimately rusted and rotted, requiring a replacement building. (Courtesy of History Center, San Francisco Public Library.)

The first pool building in Larsen Park was later named for Charlie Sava in 1981. Sava, a legendary swimming instructor who coached swimming at the Crystal Plunge pool for 20-plus years, was a member of the Dolphin Club and coached the 1936 US Olympic swim team. Later, a replacement building was constructed, and his name was carried over to the state-of-the-art structure. (Courtesy of History Center, San Francisco Public Library.)

The Balboa Park pool was dedicated in 1958. The event featured an exhibition by local swimming star Ann Curtis Cuneo, who won Olympic medals in the sport and broke aquatic records. The pool was part of a recreation program where children could be taught to swim and learn about water safety. The International-style facility was designed by architect Frederick Reimers. (Courtesy of San Francisco Recreation and Park.)

Tennis started in Golden Gate Park in 1901, with the park's first tournament played on what were eight standard courts (one reserved exclusively for "ladies") and two special courts for children, all initially in clay. Shown in the background of this 1909 photograph is the first 20-foot-by-40-foot clubhouse with six showers. The courts have a reputation as a hatching ground for top tennis champions. (Author's collection.)

The bygone square-form Kezar Tennis Stadium (located above the stadium) in Golden Gate Park was built in 1924 to hold 4,400 tennis spectators. It contained two courts, one of grass and the other asphalt. Exhibition games for its dedication included local celebrity players Helen Jacobs, William "Little Bill" Johnson, and Helen Wills. The arena was removed around 1938 making way for automobile parking. (Courtesy of San Francisco Recreation and Park.)

Various activities including tennis and basketball courts are seen in this 1930s photograph of Funston Playground, now called Moscone Recreation Center. Additionally, the tot play area was located here. These courts remain today on the west end of the park, while the Marina Branch of the San Francisco Public Library was built later where the photographer was standing. (Courtesy of San Francisco Recreation and Park.)

Originally called Ortega Playground, John P. Murphy Playground was developed on a sloping sandscape. The initial work was part of the Depression-era WPA program, which funded construction of four courts. This work occurred sometime in the latter half of the 1930s. In 1941, the playground was renamed for Murphy, a painting contractor who served as a member of the park commission. (Courtesy of San Francisco Recreation and Park.)

Shown here is the original incarnation of Noe Valley Courts, which got its name from the three tennis courts built there. Previously, this was the site of the Noe Valley Primary School, which was completed about 1904. The school building became surplus, and by 1939, the WPA finished construction of the playground, which also had a play area and a convenience station. (Courtesy of History Center, San Francisco Public Library.)

In 1922, the six-acre area now known as the Presidio Wall Playground was acquired within the Presidio by the playground commission on a 99-year permit from the US government. Congressman Julius Kahn assisted in the acquisition process, and the playground was posthumously named for resident Kahn. However, it came to light that he coauthored the Mitchell-Kahn Chinese Exclusion Act of 1902, and the name was revoked. (Courtesy of History Center, San Francisco Public Library.)

This tennis clubhouse in Golden Gate Park was named for William M. Johnson, a US representative to the Davis Cup Challenge during 1920–1927 with a record 13 wins and 3 losses. A plaque there was dedicated in 1965 to James Arthur Code, a native San Franciscan and pioneer of tennis. The building was designed by architect Leonard Mosias and was dedicated in 1959. (Courtesy of History Center, San Francisco Public Library.)

One of the court sports played at Mission Playground and Pool was volleyball. This early photograph, taken in the 1930s, depicts girls playing an informal game on a hard surface court that was right next to the clubhouse where a building addition sits today. (Courtesy of History Center, San Francisco Public Library.)

Shown here is another photograph of a volleyball game that was also taken at the Mission Playground and Pool later, possibly in the 1980s. In the background is Valencia Street, and court lighting is now evident allowing for nighttime games. (Courtesy of History Center, San Francisco Public Library.)

Harking back in time to swordsmanship, the recreation department hosted classes in the sport of fencing. It was one of the first sports to appear in the ancient Olympics. The rigidly specific skill gave young people a chance to experience focus and movement skills. The sport was especially popular in physical education curriculum in the second quarter of the 20th century. (Courtesy of San Francisco Recreation and Park.)

This photograph appears to be a demonstration of field hockey to a group of onlookers. It was taken in the Potrero District's Jackson Playground with the intersection of Seventeenth and Wisconsin Streets in the background. (Courtesy of History Center, San Francisco Public Library.)

This 1924 photograph shows the fourth green of the golf course in Lincoln Park. This was 10-years after the Lincoln Park Golf Club was established. In the distance is El Camino del Mar, a scenic boulevard that wound above the steep cliffs looking out onto the Golden Gate Strait. The building in the distance was part of the adjacent Fort Miley military hospital. (Courtesy of San Francisco Recreation and Park.)

Mayor Elmer E. Robinson dedicated the 10-acre pitch-and-putt golf links in Golden Gate Park to the cry of "fore" in 1951. Golf course architect John Fleming, superintendent of golf courses for the city, transformed the park's former rolling sand dunes into green links. The nine-hole, par-three course is a short but challenging layout. (Courtesy of History Center, San Francisco Public Library.)

As shown here in the 1940s, bocce ball courts have existed in Joe DiMaggio Playground (formerly North Beach) for decades. Today, a trio of courts are named to honor John J. DiMassimo, a gardener at the playground. The named courts were dedicated by Mayor George Christopher in 1961, and a bronze plaque was added to honor DiMassimo's diligence. (Courtesy of San Francisco Recreation and Park.)

Part of work done to develop Stern Grove, from 1935 through 1936, during the Depression era, was the construction of various elements for family and community activities. Some of the work done was building retaining walls, gutters, tennis courts, lawn bowling greens (shown here), barbecues, horseshoe pitching courts, children's play area, putting green, and toilet building. Repurposed basalt cobbles, boulders, and brick were used. (Courtesy of History Center, San Francisco Public Library.)

The action is intense during this scene from a girls' basketball game. This was just one of the many active recreation programs offered by the recreation and park department, which continues today. (Courtesy of History Center, San Francisco Public Library.)

Here, players are participating in a game of soccer. The recreation and park department did not have any dedicated soccer facility until Matthew J. Boxer Stadium was created in 1953 within Balboa Park. The bleachers were added in 1958, allowing a spectator seating capacity of 3,500 attendees. Boxer was instrumental in the stadium's creation, and it was named for him in 1994. (Courtesy of History Center, San Francisco Public Library.)

One of the several activities available during the mid-century in the Rossi Playground annex was the sport of horseshoe pitching. Known colloquially as barnyard golf to some, horseshoes are especially satisfying when one gets a ringer. But holding the shoe just right is a challenge to be met. Pits could be found in Stern Grove as well as Golden Gate Park. (Courtesy of History Center, San Francisco Public Library.)

In 1927, five horseshoe pits were installed in Golden Gate Park, where there was previously a rock quarry. The site was further developed in 1934 as a Depression-era WPA venture. The bas relief horse was sculpted by Jesse Sylvester Anderson, who was a cartoonist and caricaturist for the *Detroit Free Press* and later became well known while with the *New York Herald Tribune*. (Courtesy of History Center, San Francisco Public Library.)

From the early days, horse riding in Golden Gate Park used to be a common sight. A 1927 article in the *Chronicle* newspaper noted the park to have "twenty miles of bridle paths" at the time. In 1939, four concrete buildings with glass block windows and terra-cotta tile roofs were completed as a WPA project to board horses but are closed today. (Courtesy of History Center, San Francisco Public Library.)

Here, Raymond Kimbell, general manager of the recreation and park department from 1958 to 1963 (far right), tries his hand at fishing in Lake Merced Park. In 1939, the city agreed for the first time to permit boat fishing, and the lake was stocked with bass. By 1950, there were calls to limit where and when someone could fish due to the sport's popularity. (Courtesy of History Center, San Francisco Public Library.)

The basement level of the Senior Center in Golden Gate Park has a large room where several activities can take place. Here, senior participants are led in exercises. The building was first dedicated in 1932 as the Golden Gate Park District Police Station, and in 1937, its use was changed to be the San Francisco Police Academy, which lasted through 1963. (Courtesy of History Center, San Francisco Public Library.)

There was plenty of action in 1987 for the umpires to oversee in Kezar Pavilion in Golden Gate Park. The San Francisco Summer Open Table Tennis Tournament was sponsored by the San Francisco Table Tennis Club and the Recreation and Park Department. This was preceded days earlier by a group of nationally ranked players in exhibition. (Courtesy of History Center, San Francisco Public Library.)

Six

SPECIAL PLACES

Standing in front of the Conservatory of Flowers in Golden Gate Park was this fountain. The bronze statue, created in 1904, is of a boy with a tortoise at his feet. The fountain was a commission by sculptor M. Earl Cummings, who also sat on the park commission as their mandated artist who oversaw all aesthetic decisions for the city's parks. The fountain no longer exists. (Author's collection.)

Public museum patron and *Chronicle* newspaper owner Michael H. de Young long collected the spoils of many different past wars, including artillery. An unknown young sailor is shown sitting alongside the steps to the original main entry to the Memorial Museum in Golden Gate Park. This was taken in late 1918, just as the guns of World War I were being silenced in far off Europe. (Author's collection.)

Prayerbook Cross in Golden Gate Park, dedicated in 1894, was designed by architect Ernest Coxhead. It was the idea of Bishop William Ford Nichols, the second Episcopal bishop of California, to create the piece, and he found donor George William Childs, owner and editor of the *Philadelphia Public Ledger* newspaper. Childs was a philanthropist who donated many monuments to cities in the United States and England. (Author's collection.)

Spanning the south side of Stow Lake in Golden Gate Park is a double-arch structure that is clad in massive red natural boulders. Stone for the Rustic Bridge came from a quarry located near Laguna Honda, and the work was carried out by stonemason Donald McKay. To aid construction, dams were built on either side of the construction site. The bridge was finished in 1893. (Author's collection.)

This 1936 photograph is of a boy perched on one of the two facade fountain pools that were part of the original Steinhart Aquarium in Golden Gate Park. The wall-mounted walrus head spouts water, while crabs adorn the pool's edge. When the complex was rebuilt and dedicated in 2008, one of the walrus heads was saved and installed in an exhibit in the interior subterranean level. (Author's collection.)

In 1892, George M. Greene built the Trocadero, named so to evoke the famous Parisian gardens. The stick Eastlake-style two-story building, topped with a cupola and flagpole, housed a hotel surrounded by cabins. After the turn to the 20th century, a series of operators leased the resort. Later, the area became part of Sigmund Stern Grove, a gift of Rosalie Stern. (Courtesy of San Francisco Recreation and Park.)

The wood-and-glass Conservatory of Flowers in Golden Gate Park was opened in 1877. It was a gift of a group of donors who happened upon an unusual situation. In 1876, philanthropist James Lick died, leaving a large and still-crated greenhouse on his San Jose estate. The donor group purchased the kit-of-parts and donated it to the park. (Courtesy of History Center, San Francisco Public Library.)

Unveiled originally in the center of Portsmouth Square in 1897 is a monument that remembers author Robert Lewis Stevenson, who stayed in the city for a year. Bruce Porter and Willis Polk designed the granite-and-bronze monument, while the bronze ship, with its sails fully extended, was modeled by George Piper. Later, the monument was moved toward the northwest corner. (Courtesy of History Center, San Francisco Public Library.)

Birch Lake at Camp Mather was an excavation site to supply gravel for the Hetch Hetchy Dam project. Underground springs were struck during excavation, and the hollow flooded. The resulting pond was used to aid in removal of tree bark prior to the sawing process. The dam was completed in 1923, so the construction camp was no longer required for its original purpose. (Courtesy of History Center, San Francisco Public Library.)

This photograph shows one of the some two-dozen original wood cabins at Camp Mather where family memories are made. The municipal camp was a project of supervisor Margaret Mary Morgan, the first woman elected to the board of supervisors. On June 16, 1924, the board approved the name "Margaret Maryland Municipal Camp Ground," and Mayor James Rolph Jr. signed the ordinance on June 20. (Courtesy of History Center, San Francisco Public Library.)

ORIENTAL TEA GARDEN
SAN FRANCISCO GOLDEN GATE PARK
Moulin Studios

The wood Torii gate, shown here during World War II, stood in the Japanese Tea Garden in Golden Gate Park until 2001, when it was removed due to rot in the base. Concessionaire Makoto Hagiwara commissioned it around 1913 to be built at the top of a steep stairway, which made for a dramatic sight. Today, its remnants sit in a storage yard awaiting potential restoration. (Author's collection.)

In Golden Gate Park is the Portals of the Past monument, which once stood as the entry to Nob Hill's Towne Mansion. Its name comes from the following quote of the time after the 1906 Earthquake and Fire: "This is the portal of the past—from now on, once more forward." Poet (and later editor of *Sunset* magazine) Charles Kellogg Field found and immortalized this quote. (Author's collection.)

The Marina Green Yacht Harbor lighthouse was constructed in 1931. Stone for the tapered octagonal building was salvaged from the burned Pacific Heights residence of George A. Pope. Its illumination source was a 1,000-watt fixture, which is normally used in an airport, and it was automated. The light's two glass colors were red, indicating portside, and green on the harbor side, indicating starboard. (Courtesy of San Francisco Recreation and Park.)

The Whales sculpture was a favorite at the California Academy of Sciences in Golden Gate Park. It was a commission sculpted by Robert B. Howard for use at the Golden Gate International Exposition's San Francisco Building on Treasure Island in 1939. In 1956, a portion of it was installed in front of the park's aquarium, but it was removed to storage in 2004. (Courtesy of History Center, San Francisco Public Library.)

In 1959, the three-acre Storyland exhibit debuted at the San Francisco Zoo, bringing the places in classic children's stories to life. This one portrays the rhyme about the "Old Woman in a Shoe." Others included Humpty Dumpty, the witch's gingerbread house from Hansel and Gretel, Rapunzel's Castle, and a scene of giant mice pulling Cinderella's pumpkin coach. The attraction was removed in 1996. (Courtesy of History Center, San Francisco Public Library.)

Bison originally roamed free on the American Plains. They were first introduced into Golden Gate Park in 1891 as the beginning of what would become over time a collection of creatures of varying kinds. In 1929, the San Francisco Zoological Gardens, today's zoo, was established to house the city's growing collection, but the bison remained in the park under the zoo's care. (Courtesy of History Center, San Francisco Public Library.)

In 1943, a model barnyard was opened in Golden Gate Park as part of the Sharon playground. It contained a few farm animals. The idea was to give World War II–era city children a familiarity with where their food came from. The exhibit consisted of a scaled-down barn structure topped by a cupola with a dovecote. The barn remains today. (Courtesy of History Center, San Francisco Public Library.)

In 1972, the monumental bronze of Col. Don Juan Bautista de Anza was placed in Justin Herman Plaza. It was a 1967 gift of Mexico's State of Senora and was temporarily placed in the San Francisco Civic Center. The sculptor was Julian Martinez, and it was cast at the Moises del Aguila Foundry in Mexico City. In 2003, the statue was moved to Lake Merced. (Courtesy of History Center, San Francisco Public Library.)

Built around 1900, the two-story octagonal Sunnyside Conservatory was part of a private estate that, at its largest, consisted of nine lots. It was granted city landmark status in 1975 as San Francisco Historical Landmark No. 78. But with the threat of demolition, the city purchased the building in 1980 for public use. In 2009, the building and grounds underwent a $4.2 million rehabilitation. (Courtesy of History Center, San Francisco Public Library.)

Free public performances of various kinds have been a staple in Sigmund Stern Grove since its dedication in 1932. The enduring direction of the annual festival, a nonprofit, has stayed in the hands of the Stern descendants since its beginning. Rosalie (Meyer) Stern chaired the festival she founded in 1938 until her death in 1956. Today, Douglas E. Goldman, Stern's great-grandson, is the chairman. (Courtesy of San Francisco Recreation and Park.)

One of the attractions at the San Francisco Zoo was this Southern Pacific Railway steam locomotive, which was built in 1924 by the Lima Locomotive Works of Ohio. It was smaller than a normal locomotive as it was only used to move cars within the rail yards. In 1957, it was retired and donated to the zoo until 1981, when it was scrapped. (Courtesy of History Center, San Francisco Public Library.)

A 26-foot-high carved totem, titled "Goddess of the Forest," was placed in Golden Gate Park in 1941. It was created by wood sculptor Dudley C. Carter for the Golden Gate International Exposition. Due to exposure to the elements, the sculptor had it moved to City College of San Francisco in 1986, shown here. Its large concrete pedestal remains in Lindley Meadow today. (Courtesy of History Center, San Francisco Public Library.)

A major new exhibit opened at the San Francisco Zoo in 1985 that was named the Thelma and Henry Doelger Primate Discovery Center, which was designed by architect Cathy Simon of Marquis Associates. The total cost of $7 million from private donors was shored up with funding of $100,000 appropriated by the city. The five-story-high enclosure housed 84 animals of 16 species. (Courtesy of San Francisco Recreation and Park.)

Untitled, this giant bronze egg-form full-figure sculpture is sited in Boeddeker Park. It was created in 1985 by sculptor Anthony J. Smith to celebrate the Tenderloin's diverse cultures, ethnic groups, and ages with inset representations of 14 faces. The masks represent residents, including the park's namesake, Fr. Alfred Boeddeker. In 1986, the sculpture was dedicated. (Courtesy of History Center, San Francisco Public Library.)

Seven

EVENTS

The Presidential Tally ho Party—President McKinley in Golden Gate Park, San Francisco, California. Copyright 1901 by Underwood & Underwood.

Pres. William McKinley made a weeklong visit in May 1901 to San Francisco. He is pictured as part of a Tally Ho Party in Golden Gate Park. He also broke ground for the Dewey Monument in Union Square and created a special bond with San Francisco's citizens as the first sitting president to visit San Francisco. Four months later, McKinley died of an assassin's gunshot. (Author's collection.)

The civic center is shown here in 1948. Note that there are four one-story buildings, which are a remnant of temporary barracks, used as lodging for visiting military personnel during World War II. The 55 White Company busses seen at the center are being displayed as new replacements to streetcar lines. After being displayed at the center, the busses paraded along Market Street. (Courtesy of San Francisco Recreation and Park.)

The Raymond Kimbell Playground was originally part of Hamilton Square, established in 1855, but the south side was sold off. With redevelopment of the Western Addition, some of the property was reacquired. A fieldhouse and fields were constructed. This shows the 1965 dedication to honor recreation and park general manager Raymond Kimbell, who was retired but had spent much effort on Hamilton Square. (Courtesy of San Francisco Recreation and Park.)

John McLaren Park was dedicated in 1927, but it was just the beginning of a long gestation period. A major addition came when Louis Sutter Playground was dedicated on May 4, 1967. Sutter is shown at right. The playground was in the park's northeast corner. Sutter was former president of the recreation and park commission between 1951 and 1957. (Courtesy of History Center, San Francisco Public Library.)

The showcase event called Bike-O-Rama took place in 1968 in Golden Gate Park. Here, girls on unicycles demonstrated the balance needed for this sport. This was during a period focused on getting people out of their cars and onto bicycles. This was the beginning of providing specific pathways for bicycle recreation. The park's John F. Kennedy Drive was just closed on Sundays as an experiment. (Courtesy of History Center, San Francisco Public Library.)

Within the Bay View Playground, first opened in 1925, was the Martin Luther King Jr. Swimming Pool, which was originally an open-air pool. Shown here is the Olympic-size pool that was opened on August 3, 1968, commemorating the civil rights leader who was slain the previous April. Today, there is a replacement indoor pool on the site. (Courtesy of San Francisco Recreation and Park.)

In 1968, a new program was started at the Marina Yacht Harbor. Called Come Sail with Me, it exposed children from recreation centers and clubs to boating. The mission encouraged minority youngsters to reach for higher goals. Sponsored by the San Francisco Yacht Club, members brought children onto their boats. The following year, the adjacent St. Francis Yacht Club hosted the event. (Courtesy of History Center, San Francisco Public Library.)

In 1968, a new recreation program commenced that was intended to inspire youngsters in low-income areas. Called Tennis for Everyone, it exposed children to the sport. Local tennis star Rosemary "Rosie" Casals, later inducted into the International Tennis Hall of Fame and a resident of the Western Addition, teamed with other tennis professionals to show Hunters Point children her bravura. (Courtesy of San Francisco Recreation and Park.)

An unusual play element in Mission Dolores Park was a dory. It was a gift from the US Navy's *Coral Sea* ship and was dedicated in a ceremony held on November 6, 1975. It remained in place until 2011, when there was a major park rehabilitation. Another remains in a Golden Gate Park playground near the intersection of Forty-fifth Avenue and Lincoln Way. (Courtesy of History Center, San Francisco Public Library.)

In 1974, new playground equipment was installed in Bay View Playground. Later, on December 22, 1976, a decommissioned F-8 jet plane was installed augmenting the play equipment, a donation of the USS *Coral Sea* naval carrier ship. The jet was helicoptered across San Francisco Bay from Alameda Naval Air Station to nearby Candlestick Park and then towed to the playground. (Courtesy of History Center, San Francisco Public Library.)

Daniel Koshland Park was dedicated on June 30, 1977, his 80th birthday. The two-parcel property opened with two play areas, an arbor, basketball court, a small amphitheater, and in-ground slides. Dan Koshland, lower left, (1892–1979) was a civic leader, philanthropist, and businessman (Levi Strauss and Company's chief executive officer) whose legacy was a guiding light for those working for positive social change. (Courtesy of History Center, San Francisco Public Library.)

At the center of Washington Square is a smaller than life-size cast pewter likeness of Benjamin Franklin. It was originally dedicated elsewhere in 1879 and funded by Dr. Henry Cogswell. After being cleaned, this shows it being remounted. It was rededicated on April 22, 1979. The event included a 100-year-old time capsule that was opened revealing a variety of period items. (Courtesy of History Center, San Francisco Public Library.)

The high-density, low-income Tenderloin District has always required more open space for residents. The corner property of Sgt. John Macaulay Park was dedicated on February 22, 1983, by Mayor Dianne Feinstein, with Macaulay's mother and brother in attendance. The naming was to honor the slain police officer who died in September 1982 and was posted at the nearby Northern Police Station. (Courtesy of History Center, San Francisco Public Library.)

The two-story property that became the Mission Recreation Center was constructed in 1924 and used by a variety of business over time, including a laundry. The first rehabilitation phase, a 35,000 square-foot gymnasium, was opened by Mayor Diane Feinstein in 1984. The balance of the building, a community center, was opened in 1985 with meeting rooms, library, and an auditorium. (Courtesy of History Center, San Francisco Public Library.)

Golden Gate Park was the site of a celebration held in Speedway Meadow (now Hellman) on March 7, 1981, to celebrate Arbor Day, a traditional special day to plant trees. The mission was to highlight the role of citizens in planting trees and especially for children to learn about renewal and reforestation of the city's many parks and its natural environment. (Courtesy of History Center, San Francisco Public Library.)

Queen Beatrix of the Netherlands (shown far right) visited the Dutch Windmill in Golden Gate Park on June 22, 1982. She was there to see the garden named for her grandmother Queen Wilhelmina. The garden's naming took place in December 1961 when the Netherlands Counsel General helped to plant some 5,000 tulip bulbs that had been donated by Associated Bulb Growers of Holland. (Courtesy of History Center, San Francisco Public Library.)

Mayor Dianne Feinstein is shown alongside Fr. Alfred Boeddeker during a ceremony in Boeddeker Park, located in the Tenderloin District. Originally named Central City Park, the park was officially renamed for Boeddeker on January 19, 1984. Boeddeker (1903–1994) was made pastor of the Tenderloin District's St. Boniface Church in 1949 and was founder of the St. Anthony's Dining Room in 1950. (Courtesy of History Center, San Francisco Public Library.)

The softball field at Glen Canyon Park was named Thelma Williams Softball Diamond by the recreation and park commission in January 1991. Williams was a volunteer at the park for the previous 15 years and elsewhere in the city for some 20 years prior to that. Her untiring contribution was to teach children the fundamentals of baseball; she died in 2000. (Courtesy of History Center, San Francisco Public Library.)

In Golden Gate Park is McLaren Lodge where a tree has a cult status, especially during the holiday season. Uncle John's Tree, a Monterey cypress, was first lit in 1930 with 800 light bulbs. The tree was so high that fire department ladders were used to aid the decorating. This photograph recorded the annual event on December 12, 1990. (Courtesy of History Center, San Francisco Public Library.)

Eight

Before or During Development

Today's Francisco Park has its roots in having been one of the city's earliest reservoirs, which was fed from Lobos Creek. Eventually, the Spring Valley Water Company purchased it, which was purchased, in turn, by the city in 1930. The reservoir ceased to be used by 1941 and sat unused until 2022, when it was landscaped and dedicated as a new park. (Courtesy of San Francisco Municipal Transportation Authority Photo Archive.)

This c. 1900 shot shows the property owned by Gray Brothers Crushed Rock Company, which used it for quarrying operations on Corona Heights. The quarrying left gaping scars in the hilltop landscape. The company made brick in the three-story factory's 28-compartment kiln with 160-foot-high chimney. In 1937, the property was purchased by the city to become States Street Playground, a portion of several contiguous recreation properties. (Courtesy of Greg Gaar.)

After the 1906 Earthquake and Fire, South Park, like so many open spaces in the city, became a camp for refugees. Ultimately, 19 wood two-story buildings were constructed there as part of Camp No. 28. The official camp opened in December 1906, and at its height, it housed 648 people. It was closed in 1908, and the buildings removed. (Courtesy of San Francisco Recreation and Park.)

Here, mosaics are being prepared for installation on walls of the first-floor lobby of the Beach Chalet Building in Golden Gate Park. During 1936, and through the following year, artist Primo Caredio executed installation to the designs by Lucien Labaudt, who also painted frescos on the walls around the mosaics. Some of the walls are still in their preparation stage for painting. (Courtesy of San Francisco Recreation and Park.)

Located in San Mateo County, Sharp Park was the product of extended court litigation with many twists. Honora Sharp, the widow of George F. Sharp, died in 1905 and bequeathed $200,000 to the park commission. Not until 1917 did the Sharp's seaside San Pedro Ranch property, which was farmed for artichokes, finally get into the commission's hands as compensation in lieu of the cash. (Courtesy of San Francisco Recreation and Park.)

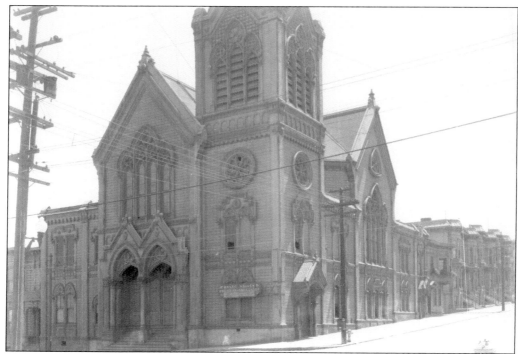

Originally dedicated in 1885 as the Simpson Memorial Church, the Victorian building was no longer used by the beginning of the Great Depression. It became the needed recreational center that was financed by citizen Adolph Rosenberg. The building's renovation into the Hayes Valley Recreation Center, which opened in 1930, included a basketball court, clubrooms, and a camera room. (Courtesy of San Francisco Recreation and Park.)

Gilman Playground, previously known as Gilman Beach, when this photograph was taken, was the only public park located right on San Francisco Bay and not near the Golden Gate Strait. Picnicking and boating were its main attributes in the early years. Later, much of the water would be filled-in for construction of Candlestick Park. (Courtesy of San Francisco Recreation and Park.)

The Glen Canyon Park recreation center, seemingly a grouping of several buildings attached together, is under construction in this c. 1937 photograph. The recreation center contained a community theater, gymnasium, and many other related spaces. Additionally, there were improved tennis and volleyball courts as well as a baseball field. The cost of $214,277 was carried out as a project of President Roosevelt's WPA. (Courtesy of History Center, San Francisco Public Library.)

One of the large masses of the WPA-built complex is the gymnasium in Glen Canyon Park recreation center, which is shown here under construction around 1937. The space is illuminated by clerestory windows, and the walls were paneled in vertical wood boards. (Courtesy of History Center, San Francisco Public Library.)

Shown on the left side of this 1933 photograph is the Rolph Playground with its original clubhouse, but on the right, and across Potrero Avenue, is the future site of Potrero del Sol Park, which was not dedicated until 1984. That site was occupied by the Knudsen Dairy processing facility and Acme Gravel. (Courtesy of San Francisco Municipal Transportation Authority Photo Archive.)

Before being landscaped for the new Angelo J. Rossi Playground, the site was the southwest portion of the decommissioned Odd Fellows Cemetery. Architect William Merchant envisioned a clubhouse centered on Arguello Boulevard, accessed by a pair of decorative stairways. Only the stairways were constructed by 1936, and a pool building came much later. (Courtesy of History Center, San Francisco Public Library.)

Portsmouth Square still looked like this up until 1949, when the board of supervisors approved preliminary plans for an underground garage. Protests from many parts of the city cited destruction of the park's historic character. Columnist Herb Caen sarcastically quipped that the property was being "Union Squared," referring to what had been done to the city's downtown shopping center park previously. (Courtesy of History Center, San Francisco Public Library.)

This view shows the Upper Noe Valley Recreation Center property prior to being developed. Public requests for a park located in this vicinity started in 1926. The playground department finally forged ahead in 1935 to start acquisition of as much of the already built out block as possible. In 1950, the final parcels were acquired, leaving some on the east end. (Courtesy of History Center, San Francisco Public Library.)

This aerial photograph of Funston Playground, now Moscone Recreation Center, shows the property before the branch library was constructed. It shows the state of the park just after it was restored in 1946. With World War II in full swing, the US Army commandeered use of the fields in 1942. Barracks were constructed here to augment those in Fort Mason across the street. (Courtesy of History Center, San Francisco Public Library.)

Landscaping for the St. Mary's Recreation Center is shown in process here. In March 1928, the initial parcel of land was given by the Archdiocese of San Francisco to the playground commission, which was combined with an additional purchase by the city to create the original project site. The playground was developed between 1930 and 1933 using federally funded WPA labor. (Courtesy of History Center, San Francisco Public Library.)

Sunset Playground was first opened in 1940 with a small field house, volleyball, basketball, and tennis courts. A much-larger recreation building, shown here, was built in the form of a giant Quonset hut in 1951, which was designed by architect William Merchant. The half-round form, popularized during World War II for its efficient structural capability, achieved a wide span area without columns using laminated wood trusses. (Courtesy of History Center, San Francisco Public Library.)

The purchase of many private Bayview District properties for the Joseph Lee Recreation Center was completed in 1943. Architect William Merchant's plans for the curved roof project were approved by the recreation commission in 1944. Mayor Elmer E. Robinson dedicated the new building in 1951. The U-shaped building contained a gymnasium, clubroom, auditorium with stage, offices, locker rooms, and storage. (Courtesy of History Center, San Francisco Public Library.)

The property that became the Fillmore-Turk Minipark in 1968 was a storage yard for the San Francisco Municipal Railway. This area was part of the mid-century Western Addition Redevelopment Project. The intent was to eliminate blighted conditions and was funded by the federal government's Urban Renewal Program. The building to the park's left was a powerhouse for the railway, which remains today. (Courtesy of San Francisco Municipal Transportation Authority Photo Archive.)

The two-lot property that became the Page-Laguna Minipark was purchased in 1969. The new park was dedicated in 1971 with some 100 people in attendance, including members of the Page-Laguna Neighborhood Association. Mayor Joseph Alioto attended the ceremony. Alioto championed bringing the federally funded matching dollars for the 16 initial miniparks to San Francisco; the first was named after him. (Courtesy of History Center, San Francisco Public Library.)

Construction of Fillmore-Turk Minipark was funded in 1968 by the San Francisco Municipal Railway, owner of the property. This photograph shows the park's back wall with curved front stage in the process of construction. At some point later, the property was ceded from the redevelopment agency to the recreation and park department's real estate portfolio. (Courtesy of San Francisco Municipal Transportation Authority Photo Archive.)

The dedication of Candlestick Park in 1960 on filled Bayview District land was initially to host the San Francisco Giants baseball team, and later, the San Francisco 49ers football team was added. Shown in the lower part of the photograph is what Gilman Playground looked like after filling. The diagonal row of trees denotes where the bay's original shoreline was once located. (Courtesy of History Center, San Francisco Public Library.)

This photograph, taken in early 1972, shows the upper deck expansion project of Candlestick Park. Expansion of seating (an additional 16,000 seats) was required as the 49ers football team moved from Kezar Stadium to Candlestick, but it was also thought that enclosing the stadium would help the problem of chilly winds present on the point, which it did not. (Courtesy of History Center, San Francisco Public Library.)

In the mid-1950s eight identical residences facing Selby Street were demolished to make way for the new elevated Interstate Highway 280. The upshot was vacant property right next to, and below, the highway. Here, Selby-Palou Minipark was later created in 1975 by Bidegain Landscape Company. The cost of $32,580 was shared with the nearby Palou-Phelps Minipark, which was constructed at the same time. (Courtesy of History Center, San Francisco Public Library.)

The Vaillancourt Fountain in today's Embarcadero Plaza, originally known as Ferry Building Park and then later renamed for Justin Herman, has just been constructed in this c. 1972 photograph. Its backdrop is the elevated Embarcadero Freeway, State Route 480, which was demolished in 1991. It awaits construction of the Embarcadero Center buildings that extended eastward to the edge of the park. (Courtesy of History Center, San Francisco Public Library.)

The future site of Potrero del Sol Park is shown here around 1970 after demolition of buildings. During the late 19th and into the early 20th centuries, the Mission District had many dairy distributors as pastureland was nearby. This property was partly the site of the Knudsen Dairy processing facility. The new park was dedicated in 1984. (Courtesy of History Center, San Francisco Public Library.)

In 1988, artist Johanna Poethig unveiled her mural of leader Harvey Milk on the exterior of the Recreational Arts Building in Duboce Park. She described it as Milk "in his victory pose on top of the image of himself dressed as a clown, with his beloved dog. The other figures represent activities at the center." The faded mural was painted over in 2009. (Courtesy of History Center, San Francisco Public Library.)

About the San Francisco Parks Alliance

The idea of separate nonprofit funding to assist the recreation and park department started in 1969 when Proposition A was rejected by voters. It was a proposal to incur a bonded indebtedness of $9,998,000 for additions to and improvements of the city's recreation and park system. This was proposed considering cuts to the department's budget at the time.

That year, Walter H. Shorenstein, who was president of the recreation and park commission, proposed the creation of a "friends of the park" type organization. The different funding model, using the public-private concept, would consist of community-minded business firms and individuals who could be called upon to contribute financial support to assist budget shortfalls. Board commissioner Frances McAteer was charged with working with recreation and park general manager Joseph Caverly to create the organization.

In 1971, the Friends of Recreation and Parks organization was established to develop and cultivate wide public engagement in recreational, educational, and cultural programs. Some of their first efforts included rehabilitation the long-inoperative trio of fountains in the Music Concourse and sponsor a public opera performance. This event became the annual Opera in the Park. Another project was that Mission Playground and Pool was in dire need of rehabilitation as the playground equipment was cited to have been installed in 1934. The friends was able to convince Foremost-McKesson, the locally based pharmaceutical distribution firm, to donate $10,000 for the task in 1973.

Since then, the organization had continued its mission to advocate for city parks and green spaces by changing its structure over time. The current name reflects the merger in 2011 of the organization, then known as the San Francisco Parks Trust, with the Neighborhood Parks Council. Today, the organization continues its important mission as the San Francisco Parks Alliance.

DISCOVER THOUSANDS OF LOCAL HISTORY BOOKS FEATURING MILLIONS OF VINTAGE IMAGES

Arcadia Publishing, the leading local history publisher in the United States, is committed to making history accessible and meaningful through publishing books that celebrate and preserve the heritage of America's people and places.

Find more books like this at
www.arcadiapublishing.com

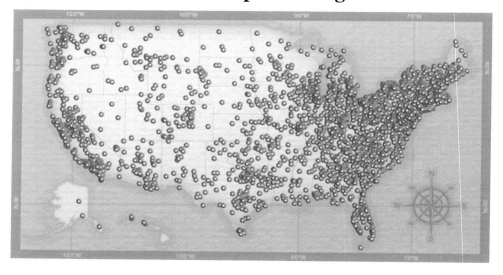

Search for your hometown history, your old stomping grounds, and even your favorite sports team.

Consistent with our mission to preserve history on a local level, this book was printed in South Carolina on American-made paper and manufactured entirely in the United States. Products carrying the accredited Forest Stewardship Council (FSC) label are printed on 100 percent FSC-certified paper.

MADE IN THE